This Walker book belongs to:

....

....

....

cock-a-doodle-doo

arf

yap

baa

neigh

mew

quack

cluck

mama

moo

splish

splash

honk

tweet

cheep

bzz

sss

oink

ree

ribbet

eek

cock-a-doodle-doo

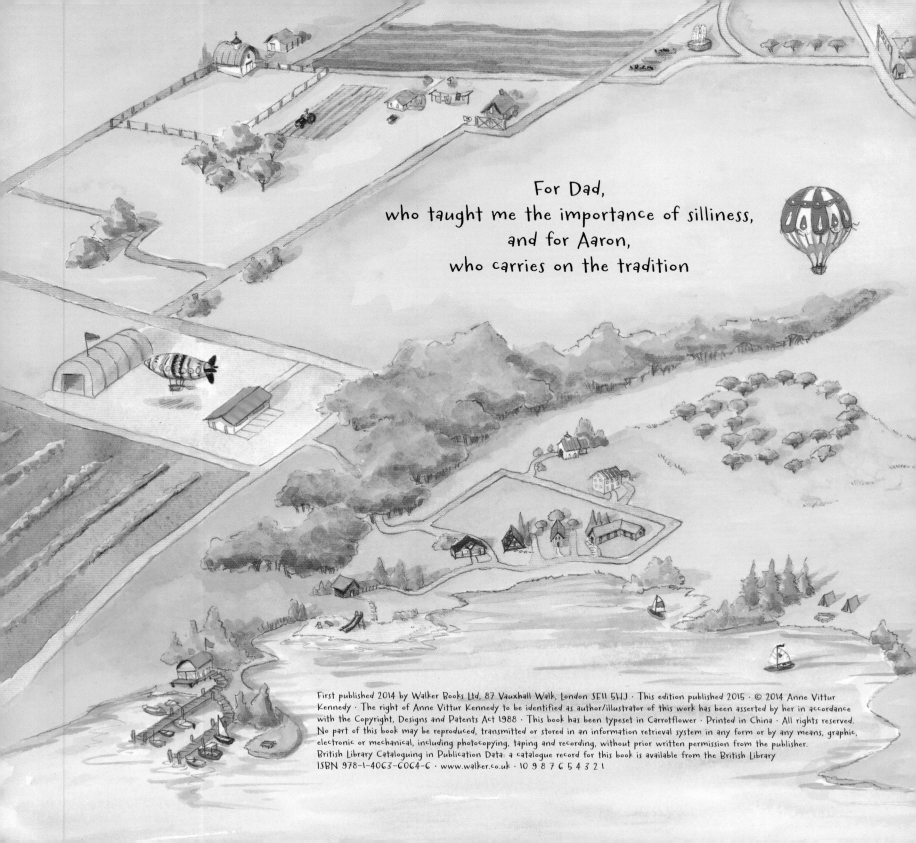

For Dad,
who taught me the importance of silliness,
and for Aaron,
who carries on the tradition

First published 2014 by Walker Books Ltd, 87 Vauxhall Walk, London SE11 5HJ · This edition published 2015 · © 2014 Anne Vittur
Kennedy · The right of Anne Vittur Kennedy to be identified as author/illustrator of this work has been asserted by her in accordance
with the Copyright, Designs and Patents Act 1988 · This book has been typeset in Carrotflower · Printed in China · All rights reserved.
No part of this book may be reproduced, transmitted or stored in an information retrieval system in any form or by any means, graphic,
electronic or mechanical, including photocopying, taping and recording, without prior written permission from the publisher.
British Library Cataloguing in Publication Data: a catalogue record for this book is available from the British Library
ISBN 978-1-4063-6064-6 · www.walker.co.uk · 10 9 8 7 6 5 4 3 2 1

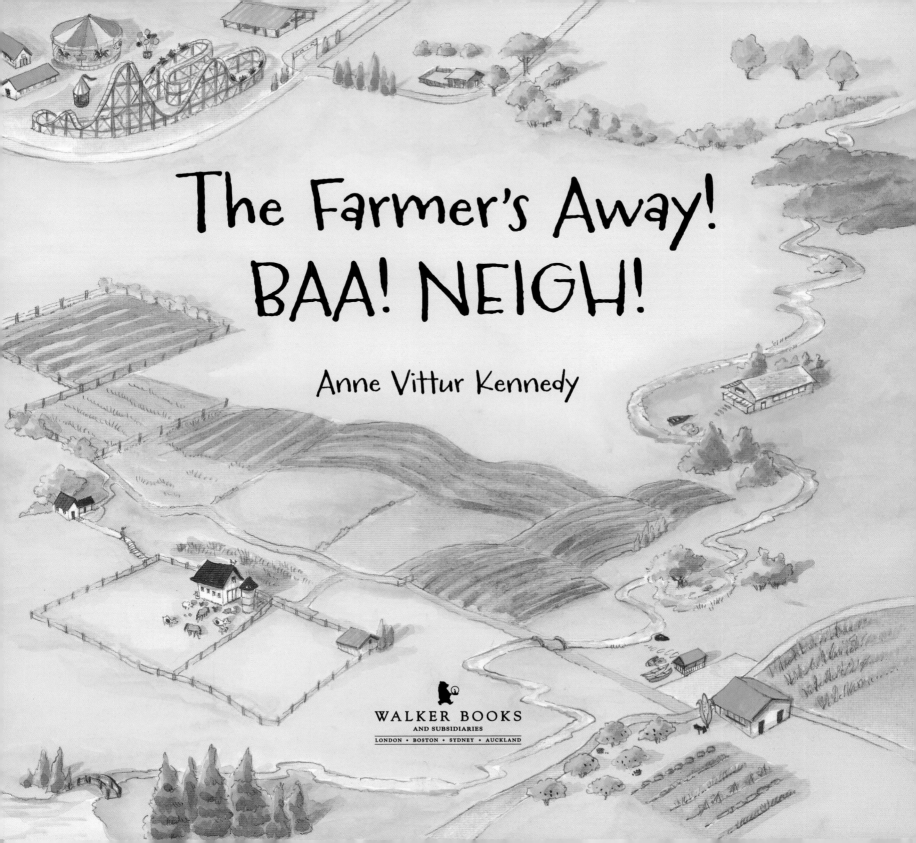

The Farmer's Away!
BAA! NEIGH!

Anne Vittur Kennedy

WALKER BOOKS
AND SUBSIDIARIES

LONDON • BOSTON • SYDNEY • AUCKLAND

ribbet mama ribbet mama
eek honk quack

splish splash baa baa
moo moo yap

arf neigh cluck cluck
cock-a-doodle-doo

mama mew mama mew
splish neigh moo

sss sss sss sss
yap sss eek

bzz bzz bzz bzz
quack bzz tweet

cock-a-doodle-doo moo
ribbet ribbet sss

baa cheep baa cheep
oink oink bzz

hmm . . . hmm . . .

neigh arf neigh moo
mew mew mew

neigh neigh baa baa
moo moo tweet

honk honk oink oink
arf cheep eek

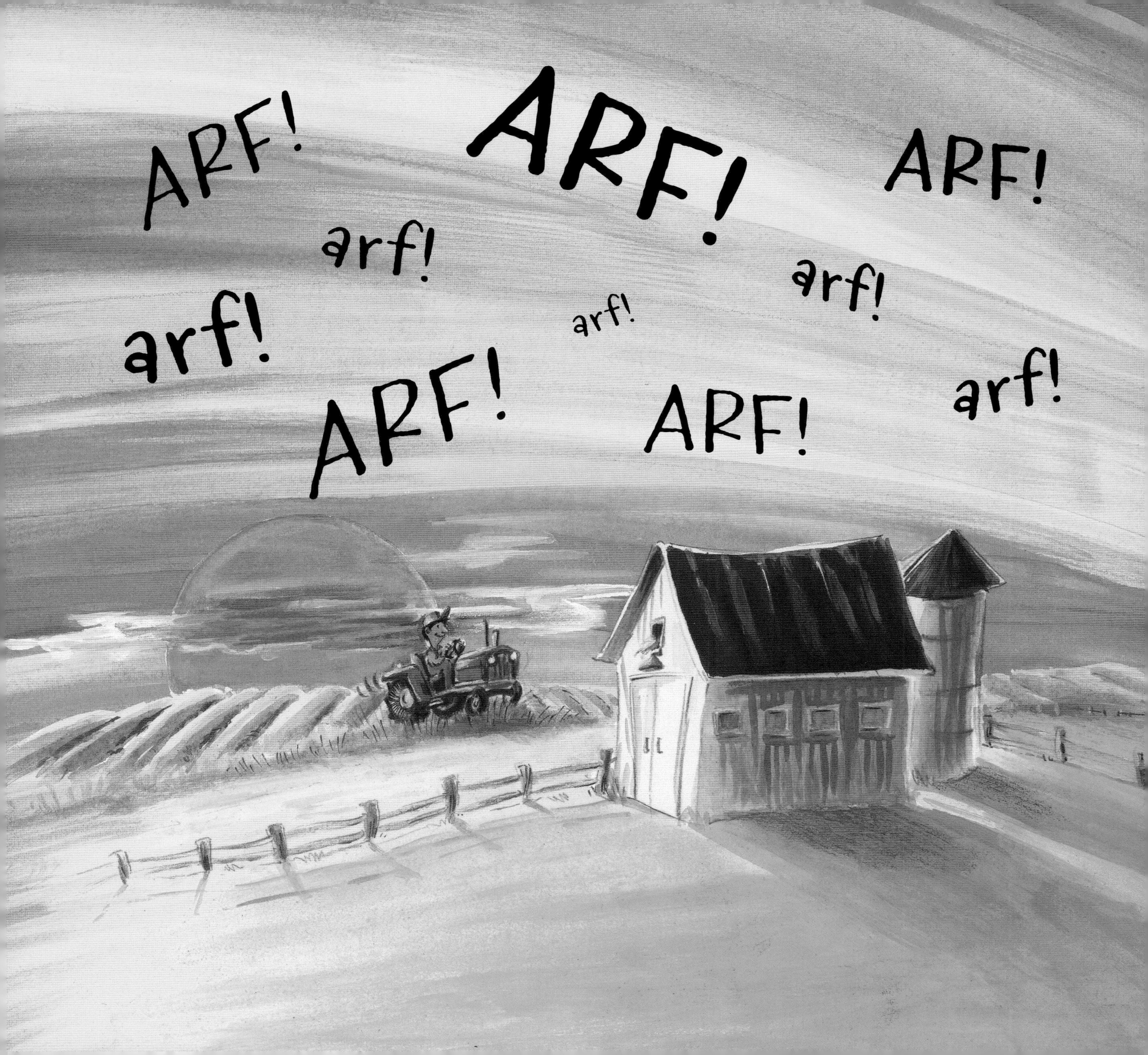

ARF!
ARF!
ARF!
arf!
arf!
arf!
arf!
ARF!
ARF!
arf!

shh shh shh shh
shh shh shhhhhhhh

shh shh shh shh
shh shh shhhhhhhh

eek!

arf

yap

neigh

baa

mew

quack

cluck

mama

moo

splish

splash

honk

tweet

cheep

bzz

sss

oink

ree

ribbet

eek

cock-a-doodle-doo

ANNE VITTUR KENNEDY

started out as a music teacher in schools, and shifted
her focus to illustration in 1982. An award-winning
illustrator of many children's books, she now enjoys writing
as well. Anne lives in the USA near Columbus, Ohio,
with her husband, Jack, and her dog, Banjo.
Her spare time is spent on (and off!)
the farm riding horses.

neigh

www.walker.co.uk